Other poetry by

Breaking Birds:
*A chilling psychological thriller written
entirely in poetic verse.*

*Poems of Separation:
A collection of poems for falling out of love*

A collection of 50 fun, inspiring and honest poems for happy campers.

First Published 2021

Campervan

I love my little campervan
My slice of heaven here on earth
To me it is quite priceless
Despite what the Autotrader says it's worth

On my way

On my way
I don't know where
On my way
To I don't care
To where life's troubles
Get left behind
Away from stresses
Of the daily grind
On my way
I don't know where
But I know I'll know
When I get there

Life Tax

There is no expiry date
On who I want to be
No MOT to pass
To say that I am me
The world is mine to travel
To see and to explore
No set rules, no life tax
But I still want to insure
I live my life each second
Make the most of every day
I travel the path less travelled
And I'll do it all my way

Stay or go?

Rain lashing
Wind crashing
Ground sodden
Grass trodden
Wheels turning
Mud churning
Tempers fraying
Not staying

Sun shining
Perfect timing
Hope growing
Rainbow showing
Smiles starting
Not departing
Children playing
We're staying

Bongo

I have a Mazda bongo
I drive it everywhere
I pack a lot of stuff
But leave behind my cares

The Road

The road before me
            opened
            And I saw it's possibilities
   the branching
        paths
        of my life
            free
            from responsibilities
 The road before me
is long
   Not
    always
      will it be
        smooth
          But I am
   prepared to brave
 the bumps

If my own road I can choose

Green Light

I'm giving myself the green light
It's ok to not know the way
It doesn't matter if I get things wrong
It's not the end if I delay

I'm giving myself the green light
It's ok not to know it all
It doesn't matter if I make mistakes
It's not the end if I fall

I'm giving myself the green light
It's ok to think about me
It matters what I want and need
Today starts and ends with me

Breathe

Breathe
I'm here
I'm free
Where I've been
Where I need to go
None of that matters now
As I unwind
Let go
Breathe

Grateful

I was somewhere different yesterday
I was someone different
                    But I moved on
                    I started again
And I may not be at my final destination
I might not even be headed the right way
                    But I'm
                    moving
                    forward
                I'm changing
            And for that I am
        Grateful

Home

My home is by the sea
The crashing waves my lullaby
My home is by the river
The flow of water
My life-force
My home is in the mountains
The peaks my hopes and dreams
My home is in the forest
The birdsong my wake-up call
My home is in the meadow
The scent of flowers my escape
My home is wherever I want
My home is wherever I am
My home is me and my campervan

Belonging

I never belonged
        I was always out of place
                Wondering
                Lonely
                Lost
        Until I discovered
      I belonged to the stars
      And I made my home

Underneath them

Rust and dents

The wheel arches are rusted
There's a dent in the driver side
There's a tear in the upholstery
And a stain I try to hide

It isn't a good looker
No rustic wood for me
Some cheap MDF cupboards
And the lino's coming free

My bunting's old and faded
The cushion's lost its stuff
My friends say that it's ancient
That my van has had enough

But despite its aged years
And it's dents and scrapes and chips
It's my tried and trusty companion
The ultimate friend for trips

It's coated in the paint of memories
It's scrapped and chipped with fun
It's rusted though with adventure
My campervan. my number one

Roots

All my life
I was a tree
Solid dependable
But stuck in one place
Roots dragging me down
But now I realise
I'm not the tree
I am the birds
And now is my time
To fly

Breathe

Breathe
I'm here
I'm free
Where I've been
Where I need to go
None of that matters now
As I unwind
Let go
Breathe

Alive

I get into my van
And drive myself away
Leave behind my problems
They'll still be there another day

I get into my van
And find a place to rest
Somewhere new to relax
A place to feel less stressed

I get into my van
And drive along the road
I don't know where I'm going
Or what the future might hold

I get into my van
And let myself just drive
The freedom of adventure
It feels great to be alive

Discovery

In my camper van
Discovering new places
Learning to be me

Home

Camper van
Shiny new
Exciting daring exploring
Discovering brand new places
Liberating inspiring learning
Rusty Old
Home

Free

Born free
Or so they say
But soon society shackles us
Responsibilities
Commitments
Slowly tying us down
Imprisoning us
In our tiny corner
Of a massive world
And so, I drive
Rebel against
Confinement
And seek out new places
Gradually growing braver
And I discover
So many corners
I realise the scope
Of a world
So wonderful
So immense
I could explore forever
And I will
One trip
At a
Time

Finding my place

I have a camper van
Together we drive
To places new
And slowly
I find my place
In the world

Adventure

Craving freedom
Appreciating nature
Meandering roads
Purposefully driven
Endlessly hopeful
Reaching destinations
Vacationing always
Anticipating adventure
Negotiating time

5* Rating

I pulled up in my camper van
To a really splendid site
The grass was green, the sky was blue
The sun was shining bright

I pulled up in my camper van
And straight away I knew
This place was worth the rating
Of its glowing 5* review

I pulled up in my camper van
I opened up the doors
Unpacked my fold up camper chair
And felt my soul restore

I pulled up in my camper van
And breathed in the fresh air
Sat back and closed my eyes
And forgot about my cares

I pulled up in my camper van
Switched off my mobile phone
I melted into nature
And made the world my home

Take control

Each journey is a memory
Travelling through life
    Not letting it pass by
    But grabbing it by the wheel
     And taking control
    Of where you are going
    So that every moment
   Is driven with purpose
    Taking you to where
You want to go

Wandering Travels

Wandering travels
Travelling around
No destination in mind
Just wheels on the ground
Each place that I pass
Each pass I go through
Is another moment captured
A wish that has come true
Wandering travels
Travelling around
No destination in mind
Just happiness found

Drive

Drive
>Just go
>Hit the road
>No place in mind
>Enjoy the journey
>Be mindful of your path
>Savour the moments you find
>Life isn't a destination
>Life is just
>a drive

Road Trip

I want to go on a road trip
Just me myself and I
I want to climb up mountains
And sleep under new skies

I want to find adventure
And visit places new
I want to see the world
And appreciate the view

Meatballs

My van is a mini IKEA
It's like walking in the store
From the cushions on the sofa
To the rug laid on the floor
In fact it's almost perfect
There's just one small request
I wish it had a bigger kitchen
To cook the meatballs I love best

Life in a van

Van life
It's not always easy
Not always wine and camp fires
It's fixing broken toilets
And realigning tyres

Van life
Is not for everyone
Though some will call it cosy
It's really pretty cramped
And the neighbours can be nosy

Van life
It's not for everyone
But it's still worth a shot
You're guaranteed adventure
Whether you like van life or not

No Plans

Take a look around you
Soak in your new home
Chat to campers beside you
Or enjoy some time alone
Take yourself off hiking
Or enjoy a quiet book
Order a cheeky take out
Or be brave and try to cook
Snuggle down in sleeping bags
Or sleep beneath the stars
Drive to somewhere near
Or journey wide and far
There is no right way to do it
No set way, no certain plan
Just relax and enjoy it
Life in a camper van

Four Wheels

My house has four wheels
It takes me places
We make new friends
And in my camper van
       Adventure never ends

Live and Laugh

Live a little
Laugh a lot
Travel often
Cares forgot
Drive a distance
Stop a while
Unwind for the day
Relax and smile

Not so shiny

There once was a lovely camper van
All shiny and tidy and glam
But it went on some trips
And now it's a tip
                Oh I love you, my camper van

Empty

My tank is empty
So I pack up my stuff
I need to recharge

The van's tank is full
I escape to my haven
And refuel my soul

Hopes and Dreams

A van full of hopes
A van full of dreams
It's not just transport
It's more than it seems

It's exciting adventures
And camp fires at night
It's travelling the world
And seeing the sights

Much more than a van
To get from A to B
It's my secret escape
From the pressures of me

A van full of hope
A van full of dreams
It's not just transport
It's more than it seems

Rain

Why
must
it rain
so?

After
weeks
of
boiling
sun

I
must
be
camping

Happy

If I were a campervan
My seats would be well worn
       They'd be rust under my arches
       And the pop top would be torn
If I were a camper van
Well-travelled I would be
       But life would be an adventure
         And happy I would be

Could I take you away?

Could I take you away
In my campervan
A chance to just chill out?
Could I take you away
From the day to day?
And stop you missing out?
Could I take you away
For the chance to explore
And enjoy the world outside?
Let me take you away
In my campervan
I know you'll enjoy the ride

The ride

One upon a time
        I let
         myself go

                I followed
                the road
           Where it led me

And when I arrived
I realised

It wasn't the destination
        But the
        love
        of the
        ride

You best life

Life
Is short
Don't waste it
Enjoy moments
Travel new places
Love your own company
Enjoy all the world offers
Spread some happiness as you go
And know that you have lived your best life

What they said

They said
it would be too hard
That I couldn't do it alone
I needed to play it safe
To live in a solid home
But instead I travelled the world
And lived in the back of my van
It hasn't always been easy
But if I can do it, anyone can

Listen

Listen
 to the rain
          rattling
          secrets on the roof
                    Enjoy it's
                    whispered words
And laugh along with its jokes

Lessons

Lessons I learnt by the roadside
Of how to live my life
Stand proud and tall as the mountains
Don't shy away and hide

Lessons I've learnt as I'm driving
Of how to live my life
Even the smallest of acorns can grow
Don't give in, keep on striving

Lessons I've learnt on my road trip
Of how to live my life
Keep spinning those wheels, keep going
Eventually you'll get a grip

Lessons I've learnt by the camp site
On how to live my life
Don't be afraid to fly from your nest
Even baby birds learn to take flight

Leaves

In the shade of the trees
I breath in
Safe in the embrace
Of leaves not yet fallen
Sheltered by a canopy
Of nature

Exhale

I exhale
And breath out
The tensions of life
Step out from under
The constrictions
of society

Darkness

When the darkness falls
When the sky closes in
When the weight bares down
Take your wheels for a spin

Get away from it all
Get away from the strain
Get away from the burden
Take a drive down lane

If it all gets too much
If it all overwhelms
If it all piles up
Take your life by the helm

Drive away from the worry
Drive away from the stress
Drive away from the pressure
                    To the place you love best

Van talk

The engine says keep on going
The wheels say keep turning around
The fuel tank says I am ready
Yet the van stays still on the ground

My heart says I must push onward
My body says enough is enough
My soul says it's time to break free
Yet the van still calls my bluff

Maybe it isn't my time yet
Maybe I'm not ready right now
Maybe this isn't for me yet
But I'll make my escape somehow

Worthy

Am I road worthy?
Is it just me who doubts
If I am enough?
When everyone else
Seems to be doing life better
And I wonder if I should turn back
But then I remember
That the journey
Is teaching me
To be me
So I move forward
I am
Worthy

Peace

Free to drive
To leave behind
Worries stress and daily grind

To escape for the week
Or just for the day
To get in my van
And just drive away

Untethered to tension
Liberated from strain
Steering myself away from the pain

To give myself over
For the pressures to cease
As I get in my van
                    And find a moment of peace

Pack it up

Pack up you bags
Grab all you stuff
Get away from this place
Enough is enough
Get in the van
Just drive for the day
Find somewhere to park
Find a place you can stay
Boil up the kettle
Unfold your chairs
Sit for a while
Let go of your cares

One day

One day I'll live in a campervan
And drive around the land
Mother nature will be my teacher
Her lessons I'll understand
I'll discover how to be happy
Learn how to connect with the earth
I'll find the meaning of life
Appreciate my own self-worth
My spirit will soar on this journey
My mind calm, focussed and present
And if all else fails at least I know
I'll save a fortune on the rent

Van life

Visiting new places
Adventure and disaster hand in hand
Never staying still
Learning to love the land
Investing in your camper
Finding a new way of life
Enjoying every moment

This is my **VAN LIFE**

Printed in Great Britain
by Amazon

66443750R00031